MW00915086

Shark Hunting the Beginner's Guide:

Full Guide on Shark Tooth Facts, Equipments to aid your hunt, Pointer to Successful hunt, uses and Myths & much more.

By

Tommy O. Hamm

Copyright@2023

TABLE OF CONTENTS

CHAPTER 1

INTRODUCTION

Exploring ocean beaches in search of shark teeth may prove a simple and entertaining pastime. Finding and identifying shark teeth is easy; you simply need to understand where to look. Teeth make interesting mementos and can even be worn as a necklace.

CHAPTER 2

Incredible Facts about Shark Tooth

What makes shark teeth so unique, then? The quantity of teeth a shark possesses throughout the course of its existence will surprise you, especially when compared to the quantity of teeth a human has.

Unconventional knowledge about shark teeth is presented below.

a. The Teeth Of Sharks Are Arranged In Rows.

Behind the row of permanent teeth that sharks use, there are many rows of developing teeth. Sharks, from the smallest sand sharks to the largest species, shed their functional teeth when they become fractured or loose, and the next tooth in line grows forward to take its place.

b. Human Teeth Are More Resilient Than Shark Teeth.

Shark teeth are surprisingly weaker than human teeth because they lack roots.

Shark teeth are commonly seen on the sea floor as well as swept up on beaches because they naturally fall out as sharks' jaws grow new teeth.

c. A Shark's Mouth Can Contain Tens Of Thousands Of Teeth.

When a shark loses a tooth, it is quickly replaced by a new one from the adjacent row. Sharks can lose up to fifty thousand teeth in their lifetime, making their fossilized remains some of the most common.

d. Megalodon Teeth, Though, Are The Highest In Value

The fossilized remains of sharks' teeth are widely distributed over the world. Megalodon teeth, the biggest of any shark's teeth ever found, are the most expensive of these.

e. The Biggest Shark Tooth Ever Discovered Was 7 5/8 Inches.

This teeth belongs to a Megalodon - the biggest shark to ever live - and was recovered in a southern river bed. It was 70 feet long and had four fangs that were each over seven inches in length.

f. Not All Shark Teeth Are Useful.

Non-functional teeth, present in basking sharks as well as whale sharks, are employed to filter feed, wherein the shark raises its mouth as well as sucks in minute prey items rather than chewing its meals.

g. There Are Four Different Kinds of Shark Teeth

Sharks' size and food determine which of the 4 kinds of teeth they have.

Needle-like teeth are long and narrow, which aids in grasping slippery fish.

Thicker, plate-like teeth are effective for crushing the shells of crustaceans and mollusks, making them a good adaptation for sharks that spend much of their time near the ocean floor.

Serrated teeth: in order to consume mammals, sharks like great whites and tiger sharks need to have serrated teeth.

Whale sharks, for example, have roughly 3,000 small individual teeth, yet they typically swallow their whole meals because the teeth aren't effective.

h. We Can Learn About The Past By Analyzing Shark Teeth.

Scientists can learn a lot from fossilized shark teeth, which can even be used to recognize extinct species dated millions of years ago.

i. Human Beings Used Shark Teeth as Tools

Native Oceanians and Americans both once relied on shark's teeth for a variety of purposes, including but not limited to weaponry, cooking utensils, and even writing.

j. Shark Teeth Got Their Own 'Toothpaste'

Fluoride, a natural cavity inhibitor found in (human!) toothpastes, coats the outer layer of shark's teeth.

l. The Teeth Of Some Sharks Are Sucked In.

Instead of losing individual teeth, the cookiecutter shark loses its complete lower plate at once and swallows it along with whatever it has just eaten.

Sharks are the only fish that are born with all of their teeth.

Shark pups are born with a full set of teeth and can swim far from their mother's right after birth.

m. The Upper As Well As Lower Jaws Of The Shark Movement

Sharks are unique among animals in that their upper

jaw is not permanently attached to their skulls; it can be detached during an assault.

n. Sharks' Bite Forces Exceed 18,000 Newtons

When compared to the biting force of a human, which is roughly 1,200N, a shark's bite is fifteen times stronger.

o. It Takes About 10,000 Years For Shark Teeth To Fossilize.

Shark teeth fossilize when a shark's body decays. It takes about 10,000 years for this to happen, which is why the majority of shark teeth fossils discovered today are between 65,000 and 70,000 years old.

CHAPTER 3

Some Pointer for a Successful Hunts

Ways to tell if they are present:

Keep your eyes out for triangle formations along the shoreline of a beach. While modern teeth remain white, the more prevalent fossils are of black teeth. Thinner triangles with varied degrees of sharpness are fastened to wider bases. Certain shark teeth have ragged edges and thus are bent in a certain direction, indicating the side of the shark's mouth from whence they came. Finding shark teeth requires more than just a keen eye and perhaps pruned fingers after a salt water bath; professional hunters need to dig as well as sift through all the sand. Common kitchen sieves and kitty litter scoops are sometimes used, although their fine mesh and large slats are ineffective.

So that you know where to look:

The best places to find shark teeth are on beaches, but they can be found anywhere sharks swim.   Florida; Mickler's Landing at Ponte Vedra Beach, South Carolina; Manasota Key, Casey Key, Florida; Cherry Grove Beach, North Carolina; Tybee Island, Florida; Topsail Beach, Georgia; as well as Venice Beach, Florida, which professes to the title of "Shark Tooth Capital of the World," due to its position over a deep fossil layer, are the best beaches for discovering shark teeth, in my experience.

Time of day you can easily locate them:

If the beach is refilled or even the ocean floor is dredged, additional shells as well as shark teeth are likely to show up. This may have been caused by humans or a natural occurrence following a storm. It's best to go at low tide, and sandbars and other areas where the sand is continually being rearranged by the ocean are prime locations.

Where do you call home, and are you close to the beach? Interested in nature? Is your family dynamic? Do you want them to go outside so that they can get some exercise, learn something

new, and enjoy the fresh air?
Could it be that you want to
have some cheap fun? Do
you fancy yourself an
individual with a penchant
for experiential education?
Or maybe you're just a
person who gets their kicks
out of the chase. In that case,
perhaps you'd enjoy going
on a hunt for sharks' teeth
then this guide is your best
belt

I have been having a lot of
fun lately visiting the local
beaches in search of "black
gold." Almost every beach
I've visited in Northeast
Florida has yielded shark
teeth fossils. Of course,
some sharks' teeth are nicer
than others, and then I can

generally locate a few good ones to add to my collection if I search hard enough at any given beach. Finding shark's teeth can be a fun and educational activity for the whole family, and this great guide will teach you the fundamentals. It is time to begin our hunt.

1. Choosing a Site

a. Educate yourself on the subject of shark migration. Seasonal changes trigger shark migrations both to and from certain regions. Large numbers of sharks frequenting the coasts explain the abundance of shark teeth in certain regions.

Sandbar sharks, for instance, congregate in enormous numbers off Florida's east coast in the spring because that's when they reproduce. After giving birth in the southern hemisphere, the adults make the long trek north, populating places like Delaware Bay in great numbers by early autumn.

b. Go to a beach. Find a beach that is known to have sharks and start looking for teeth. Except for bull sharks, which occasionally enter freshwater rivers that flow into the ocean, sharks can only be found in salt water. Doesn't waste time scouring the pond near your house.

Hot, humid locations like Hawaii and Florida are ideal habitat for sharks. Despite the fact that they also reside at the poles.

The coastlines of many states were at one time submerged, including those of California, Virginia, Florida, Hawaii, North Carolina, and Alabama. Due to the extensive flooding that occurred throughout the state, fossilized shark teeth have been discovered on land and in river beds. These shallow seas provided an ideal hunting ground for sharks.

c. Wait for a storm to pass. Shark teeth are among the marine debris that large storms can bring ashore. Less people will attend the beach on weekdays when conditions are less than perfect.

d. Get a head start. There will be less people there in the morning. Shark teeth will be more visible in the clearer water.

If you want to visit the beach without dealing with crowds, try going during the week.

e. Always come ready. In that amount of time, you are

unlikely to discover a single shark tooth. Plan on spending at least a handful of hours at the beach. Don't forget the sunscreen and drink if you want to enjoy your time there safely. You might bring a picnic lunch as well.

f. If you want to know where to go, you should ask a local. Some locals might be able to point out popular sites for finding shark teeth. If you are not from the area, someone who may be able to inform you which beaches get crowds and when, as well as which ones contain a lot of teeth. If you know someone who can send you in the correct place, you'll have a far better chance of discovering teeth quickly.

g. Obtain a license, if one is required. Based on what state as well as country you are seeking for shark teeth within, you might require to secure a permit before looking for fossils. Even if you don't need a license to collect shark teeth in certain regions, you never know which more you might turn up.

2. Finding Teeth

a. Become familiar with shark teeth. Shark teeth are

sharp at the tip and narrow at the base. Larger teeth can sometimes be found deeper in the water, but they are often found between 1/8" and 3/4" in size closer to the beach or coastline. The shape of certain teeth resembles a triangle with no top, while others more like the letter Y. Sharks can be tricky to identify due to the fact that their teeth look different according on their age and gender as well as where they are located in their jaws.

b. Seek out everything that's black. Black shark teeth fossils are common. These are exactly what you are likely to find near the shore. Gray or brown shark teeth are also found, but they are much less common. Both the crown and the root of a modern shark tooth are typically white, and they are extremely rare beach scavengers.

Remember that not all triangular objects are shark teeth; they could just as easily be rocks or stones.

Visit any gift shops that may be in the area of the beach. It's possible that they sell shark teeth and can show you a representation of what you're trying to find.

c. Search the shoreline and the nearby shallows. Shark teeth have a habit of floating to the surface of the sand and being easy to find. Among all the shells and rocks, it could be difficult to find. You might not find anything if you only look on the sand's surface.

d. Scrape up some of the sand near the ocean's edge.

If you don't find any teeth right away, you'll have to get down and dirty. Have some tools ready. A shovel, trowel, and bucket could come in handy. A strainer or colander may come in handy for sifting sand.

Look for raised sand and dig there. Teeth may or may not always be visible. Every time the tide comes in, new sand covers the old. Keep your hands dirty and don't worry about it.

e. Conduct a marine search.

If you're not catching anything in the surf, try the shallows. Grab a strainer and dip your hand under the water's surface to collect some silt. Dig around in the muck and see what you can unearth.

The shark teeth remain the main attraction, you may also come across some other interesting finds, such as those made from stingrays, porpoises, or crocodiles. Stunning shells are another possible treasure.

f. Think about getting scuba gear on rent. If you dive a little ways from the coast, you can explore more area and potentially uncover larger, older shark teeth.

g. Wait patiently.

Don't pass by a patch of sand without inspecting it thoroughly. Collecting sharks teeth typically demands a little of effort and persistence. Checking places more than once is prudent because new teeth could be brought in by waves. Over the course of its career, a single shark can manufacture up to 25,000 teeth, therefore there is no shortage of shark teeth.

CHAPTER 4

Tools Most Effective for Locating Shark Teeth

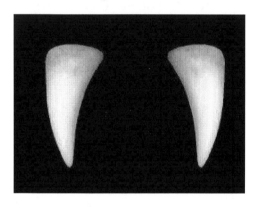

It would be great if all you needed to do to find great teeth was step outside your door and look down. Personally, I don't think so, since if the great ones were ubiquitous, nobody would want them. We really need them, and it's a challenge to track them down. There aren't many places you can go to where people will just leave their teeth lying about for you to find. A handful of these I've attended, but I usually just go to work on my teeth instead. As such, I figured I'd share my gear in case you were curious about where I get my gorgeous teeth, as that's an integral part of the sport.

1. Equipment for Collecting on Land

Precisely Crafted Sand Flea Rake

Exactly Modeled Sand Flea Rake

Featuring a sturdy construction, a sizable head, and sharp teeth, this rake is up to the task!

Digging it in will allow you to collect a large quantity of sand and sediment. The rake's basket, albeit wedge-shaped, is roomy and is roughly 16 inches across. Because it is anodized aluminum, it should hold up well in the salty ocean air.

The serrated tip of the rake also makes digging a snap. Almost all of the other implements are somewhat blunt, so you'll need to use more effort to drive them into the ground. The ergonomic shape of the handle is another nice touch. The curved shape prevents the user from having to stoop over when stirring the sediment.

Though expensive, the Exact Designs rake is money well spent.

Shovels

When searching for fossils, the shovel is the most useful instrument I have. In case you were unaware, I collect majority of the teeth I locate by digging them up myself; therefore, I require a sturdy shovel. My go-to shovel is the one on the far left. It's small and has a handle, so you can slam it hard on a vertical surface. I don't mind how short I am because I save my back from strain by kneeling or sitting when digging. A walking shovel may be seen on the right. It's just a fancy walking stick, yet it comes in convenient if you happen to stumble onto a dig site while out exploring in search of teeth. Forgive the pun, but a nice pair of gloves is essential when using a shovel. One other shovel I use when sieving is not shown; it's just a regular old garden shovel. Check the local regulations before beginning your fossil quest. A bit investigation can keep you out of legal trouble in places where it is prohibited, such as the town of Summerville, South Carolina, and the Calvert Cliffs near Maryland.

Sifter

This is yet another crucial item for any fossil hunter. Too many streams and ditches are too deep for surface collecting, but they almost certainly contain fossils that will need to be sifted out.

Destruction Man

After a certain amount of time spent excavating, you may realize that you need to shift additional soil. The devastator (known as mattocks elsewhere) proved to be the solution. I can smash through rock to get to the fossil-rich layer below with just a few swings of this powerful instrument. It has a sharp edge that can be used to sever roots. As a little of background, I can tell you that I have witnessed these in three different varieties. Wooden, hybrid wood/fiberglass, and fiberglass grips are all available. The first one I purchased was made of wood, and I used it to sweep away some roots. The master root was the name I gave it. Emotional reminiscences. To put it briefly, the story didn't make the grade. I just got a couple of weeks of use from it before the handle snapped. In general, wood is rather reliable; I must have gotten a defective handle. Not to mention, it's a fraction of the price of the fiberglass alternative. The hybrid falls in the middle in terms of price, but I have no personal experience with them and thus cannot endorse them. Anyway, I bit the bullet and got the fiberglass version, and it's been great.

A word of caution: this kind of tool should never be used on the layer itself. Any fossils that may be there will be mangled beyond recognition by you. Ensure digging is permitted in the area you intend to find fossils in, and bring shovels if necessary. For as the famous Spider-Man line goes, "With great power lies great responsibility."

Aggressive Toothiness

Here we have a sledgehammer and a prying bar that measures 17 inches in length. How could something like this be used to hunt? The procedure is as follows. Let's pretend you have a great layer smack dab in the middle of a vertical wall. The uppermost layers, including the strata, have been roasting in the sun for several days, if not weeks, and are now as hard as concrete. The sediments beneath the layer are composed up completely of fine sand, thus they are always soft (at least where I hunt). If they haven't been removed before, use your shovel to get rid of them. The result is a protruding layer on the bottom, creating an overhang. Two inches beyond the fossil layer, you put the prying bar and sledgehammer it into the wall. Soon, only the striking face will be visible. Then, you focus your energy downward. When the covering breaks apart, you can sort it by hand. All of the teeth survived the procedure unscathed since you left a 2" space between the layer as well as you inserted the bar. It's so smart it's ridiculous. That's an idea I wish I'd thought of myself. My sibling came up with the plan. Sections of collapsed walls containing fossils can be broken apart using the same approach.

Probe

Occasionally I have to search in old, unkempt ditch banks as well as creeks because I can't always search in new regions. The layer is invisible; how can you locate it? Employing a probe. To find rocks, you stick this bad boy into the ground. Then, you may simply remove the debris covering the teeth and collect them. If you need to filter through a particularly sandy area, this equipment will come in handy. When looking for gravel deposits, this is a lot more efficient method than having to remove the sand first.

Machete

Let's imagine you're digging and you locate a great layer, yet there are so many little vines and rotten roots in the way that you can't go much deeper. Voila! Unlike the devastator, the machete can precisely cut through all that trash and dispose of it. The machete is additionally handy for clearing off ground litter before you dig, as well as vines and sticker shrubs on the way to your target.

Fork

The only purpose of this instrument is to roam about and look for teeth. It's a handy walking stick that can be used to quickly turn over rocks in search of treasure. It's also the best thing ever for hauling yourself up rocky ditch banks. Simply drive it into the surface and utilize the leverage to lift yourself up. However, you can only use it to dig in sand, so if you expect to have to do any serious digging, I recommend bringing a walking shovel instead.

That's a Hammer

This is an excellent one to have around if you do any gathering in quarries. If so, you're aware that fossils are frequently unearthed in limestone and other abrasive deposits. You aren't interested in returning a two-ton rock to the truck just to get one tiny cow shark tooth, would you? You may easily use this and move on. Every time I use this equipment, I put on my safety glasses first.

Chisel

To separate fossils from their matrix with greater precision, I utilize the masonry chisel alongside with the rock hammer's hammer side. Take note of the tool's hand guard; it's an absolute necessity. It would be a bummer to cut a nice toothin' day short by bashing your hand against something. When I employ this equipment, like with the stone is hammer, I make sure to protect my eyes with protective glasses.

2. Gear for Scuba Diving

The Point-Of-Sale

The simplest way to take advantage of river diving is with an aquatic vehicle, so I sold some goods and ended up with the cash to score a watercraft. Aesthetically unpleasing and functionally ineffective. However, with the Six hp motor, I can complete the journey in 40 minutes instead of the four hours it would take paddling.

Mask

This is the bare minimum need for diving. You won't be able to see anything without a mask, so make sure to carry one. The enormous thick band on the rear is an alternative for the one the face mask originally arrived with. A slap strap, in my opinion, is an indispensable item. It's absolutely bouyant, meaning that if you misplace your mask for any reason, it might float to the surface, and it doesn't tug your hair like a regular strap would.

Fins

You can't swim against the current if you don't have fins. They additionally make you appear larger to alligators while swimming. I don't know whether that really matters, but it sure does have a good ring to it.

Gloves

The necessity of these is less evident. The riverbeds are littered with shards of glass that could easily sever a bare hand. It would not be preferable to suffer a serious cut in these vile waterways.

Exercise Belt

You'll need a lot of lead to make yourself heavier and sink to the river floor, where you'll have an easier time fighting the stream. A lot more is required of you than usual when you're going to be in salt water. Depending on the day, I'll be carrying around 30-60 pounds.

Lights

Light can penetrate to a depth of around 10 feet when the water's surface is clean (no sediment is suspended) due to the presence of tannic acid. Like being submerged in a cup of tea, no joke. If you want to see the bottom teeth, you're going to need a BRIGHT light. The left-hand light is a headlamp that serves as my primary source of illumination. With a headlight, you can keep both hands free to do whatever else needs doing. There are many more than you think! A conventional hand light, on the right, serves as a backup. Always bring a spare so that your dive won't be ruined if the primary fails.

Goodybag

You need something to corral all those 6-inch megs, right? Even though mine is quite old, it still performs admirably. Like the water, everything has been discolored by tannic acid. I know, right? I like bags that come with the wire opening since they can expand really and they are easy to fasten to you while ascending as well as descending.

Kneepads

These aren't required, but they will make your wetsuit last much longer and are highly recommended. There are sharp rocks everywhere, and you have to spend much of spare time on your knees. Wetsuits are easily destroyed by sharp rocks.

At least a single of these is required! You can't stand against the current unless you have stuff to stab into the riverbed. A screwdriver is the ideal tool for this task. However, having a tool to use when excavating underground is always a plus. A rake sounds awesome in that instance. You can additionally employ it to keep yourself in location, but its more difficult because its harder to get the three prongs through the marl. The void of features marl bottom can be navigated with these tools by marking lines of travel.

Regulator

Another essential piece of gear for underwater exploration is presented here. Don't skimp on quality because you'll be using it to breathe. Have a reliable dive shop inspect it if you decide to buy a used one. Due to its two inhalation stages, this apparatus is also known as an octopus. One has been stashed away as a backup.

The rest of my gauges are housed in a console. I've got a compass to get me around, a pressure gauge to tell me the quantity of air I have left, as well as a computer that can calculate cool stuff like my depth, decompression time, and how long I can stay at the bottom for. The use of a computer is optional but recommended.

Coveralls

Usually I don't wear a wetsuit when I go diving here because the water is so warm. Coveralls assist in shielding you from annoying small biting minnows, crabs, unintentional scrapes with pebbles, etc. However, a wetsuit is required to stay on of the coveralls when the temperature drops.

Booties

They prevent blisters on your feet from being caused by your fins. If the water is chilly, your feet will stay toasty in these.

BCD

Most of your scuba gear budget will go toward your buoyancy control device (BCD). You can store small items in the pockets, use the rings to attach clips (to which you attach your handheld tools), and use the air from the reservoir to ascend to the surface of the water when you're prepared to leave the depths. Used BCDs are available; just make sure the internal bladder is in good shape and free of punctures.

Bag

To avoid stumbling into clutter while out on the water, you'll want to bring along some sort of storage container.

Tanks

Since renting tanks required so much maintenance, I

finally gave in and bought my own so that I wouldn't have to make two journeys to a dive shop following each dive. A few years ago, I paid $200 for each of mine; today's price is likely more. Each tank must undergo a visual check annually before being filled at a dive shop. That costs money. Then, once every five years you're required to undergo a hydrostatic assessment before the dive shop can fill your tanks. A price has to be placed on that.

CHAPTER 5

Meaning Behind a Shark Tooth Pendant

The shark tooth pendant is a powerful talisman from long ago. It has been used for a thousand years by people all across the world. Polynesian and Pacific Islander peoples, as well as those who lived in coastal areas, frequently adorned themselves with shark teeth.

But what does it symbolize to wear a shark tooth necklace? There was a wide range of interpretations based on culture.

Protection

The idea that wearing a shark tooth necklace will ward off shark attacks and other water-related dangers has its roots in ancient Hawaiian mythology. According to the myth, a shark tooth adorned warrior emerged from the water after defeating a god. Because of its reputation for providing magical protection, this magical piece of jewelry is worn by many surfers and divers.

Shark teeth were traditionally hung at the front door of homes in several African cultures as a talisman against evil spirits and the evil eye. The usage of shark teeth as a form of household security in African culture was analogous to the use of a Wes

Toughness and machismo

The Maori people of New Zealand have long placed a high value on sharks. The Maori believe that a necklace made from a Mako shark's tooth will provide the wearer with the shark's virility, vitality, and manliness. These amulets were kept safe and passed down through the generations.

Best wishes

Folklore about sharks had a significant role in the lives of Fijians. Dakuwaqa, their shark-God, was a hybrid of a shark and a man. A shark tooth bracelet was thought to contain the spirit of Dakuwaqa, who gave good fortune to Fijian sailors and fisherman.

In the modern Western world, faith in ghosts and pagan deities is rather uncommon. These days, a shark necklace serves as more of an accessory than anything else. You may rest assured that the shark's sprit will be present whether you're shopping for a one-of-a-kind gift or a pendant for yourself.

Made in the USA
Columbia, SC
03 November 2024

45574300R00035